CAROLYN J. WEBB

Early Communication Pocketbook

3 Easy Steps to Enhance Your Child's Speech and Language Development in Just 7 Days!

First published by DIY Speech Therapy 2023

Copyright © 2023 by Carolyn J. Webb

All rights reserved. No part of this publication may be reproduced, stored or transmitted in any form or by any means, electronic, mechanical, photocopying, recording, scanning, or otherwise without written permission from the publisher. It is illegal to copy this book, post it to a website, or distribute it by any other means without permission.

Carolyn J. Webb asserts the moral right to be identified as the author of this work.

Carolyn J. Webb has no responsibility for the persistence or accuracy of URLs for external or third-party Internet Websites referred to in this publication and does not guarantee that any content on such Websites is, or will remain, accurate or appropriate.

Designations used by companies to distinguish their products are often claimed as trademarks. All brand names and product names used in this book and on its cover are trade names, service marks, trademarks and registered trademarks of their respective owners. The publishers and the book are not associated with any product or vendor mentioned in this book. None of the companies referenced within the book have endorsed the book.

First edition

This book was professionally typeset on Reedsy.
Find out more at reedsy.com

Contents

Foreword		iv
1	Introduction	1
2	Communication Basics	3
3	Eye Level Positions	5
4	Days 1 and 2: Eye Level Video Practice	12
5	Pausing	14
6	Days 3 and 4: Pausing Video Practice	17
7	Modeling Without Expectation	20
8	Days 5 and 6: Modeling Without Expectation Video Practice	30
9	Day 7: Pulling It All Together	33
10	Conclusion	36
11	References	38

Foreword

I hope you enjoy the 'Early Communication Pocketbook'! If you are interested in more tips you can sign up below:

GRAB YOUR FREE TIP SHEET HERE!

If you are interested in a 15 minute call with the author about coaching sessions, sign up for the Tip Sheet and you'll find a link to book your call.

Disclaimer
   Parents and caregivers are strongly advised to seek the guidance of a professional as early as possible if there are any concerns about a child's

speech, language or communication skills. This book is not intended to replace therapy or the direct support of a speech and language pathologist or therapist. Its purpose is to educate parents and caregivers as they support their child. Results are not guaranteed. A child's progress in communication will depend on many factors. This book can be a useful tool to help support parents and caregivers as a first port of call before or while attending a speech and language therapist.

Other Upcoming Books By This Author:

A Parent's Guide To Early Communication; Jump-Start Your Child's Interaction and Language Skills Towards First Words and Phrases; 7 Powerful Strategies With Transformative Video Exercises (Due for Publication December 2023)

Supporting Early Communication Through Everyday Routines; Effectively Target Speech, Language and Independence Skills in Toddlers With Easy Transformative Video Exercises (Due 2024)

Promoting Early Communication and Play; A Step-by-Step Parent Guide to Enhance Language in Toddlers and Preschoolers Through Everyday Fun Games With Transformative Video Exercises (Due 2024)

If you have any questions about this or other upcoming publications, you can contact the publisher *DIY Speech Therapy* at this email address: info@diyspeechtherapy.com.

All text is original and written solely by the author. The image on the front cover and images contained in this book have been generated with the assistance of AI.

If you enjoy this book, help other parents find it by leaving a review here:

https://www.amazon.com/review/create-review/?ie=UTF8&channel=glance-detail&asin=B0CNTYTD51

Leave a Review!

1

Introduction

Welcome to the 'Early Communication Pocketbook'! My name is Carolyn Webb and I'm extremely excited to share this book with you! For one, I get to talk about what I'm passionate about: helping parents help their own children. I can't wait to get started and give you some simple things you can do right now. These simple steps are designed to help you become the best communication partner for your child in the shortest amount of time, so that your child can have the best chance to practice and improve their interaction, communication, speech and language skills.

A little bit about myself: I'm a Speech and Language Therapist and I have worked in this area for over 30 years. So I have had a lot of opportunities to try out these (and lots of other) strategies for myself.

So if you have a child who is a late talker, a non-speaker, or just starting to use their first words, this book is for you.

I'm not going to give you a long list of bullet points for you to try to work out all by yourself. Instead, we will take a deep dive into three of the most important evidence-based strategies that make a difference. We will look at *why* they are so important, and *how* to put them into practice most effectively, so that they become a natural part of the way you interact with your child. All this within just 7 days!

You may think: 'Well, why do I need this? I use strategies all the time already!'. Yes, you do! We all do many things naturally to help support our children. But when a child is experiencing challenges in learning to communicate, there are things we can tweak in a planned or structured way that can really help to move them along.

Not only will we be demystifying some of the strategies that Speech Therapists use all the time, BUT the best part is that you will get to video yourself as you try out each strategy for yourself, with some guided written instructions. You'll also get to reflect on any changes that you see, and take away some key learning that you'll be able to put into practice into the future so that it becomes a normal part of your interaction.

As you go through the Early Communication Pocketbook, make sure to do all the exercises each day as laid out. You'll be asked to try things out that won't take more than 10 minutes a day to do, with a little reflection time afterwards.

Some of the best intentions end up in the bottom drawer… This won't happen here, as long as you follow the instructions carefully, and do the practice.

So let's jump right in!

2

Communication Basics

Let's take a quick look at some of the basics when it comes to speech and language terms we use:

Communication is a broad umbrella term for any kind of message that is sent to someone else. This could be with or without words, or it can be by using body language, facial expressions, hand signs, pictures, written text, or a device with picture icons that can be used to interact and communicate something to someone else.

When we interact with a child, we need to use a *Total Communication Approach*. This means that we accept any way that our child wishes to communicate something. We accept their first attempt and do not wait for them to ask again in a 'better' way. If they reach, look, make a sound, or pull or push you, move your hand to make something happen, or use words, these are all to be accepted as messages, as soon as you have understood their message.

Vocalization refers to any sound your child makes that is not a clear word or words. This could involve sighs, laughs, grumbles, long vowel sounds

('Aaaaah!' 'Eeeeeeh!'), singing with no words, or 'chatter' that sounds conversational but has no clear words. One of the main things about vocalizations in children who are not using words is that we forget to tune into them. We naturally tend to focus on the physical ways our children communicate and we forget the importance of vocalizations and vocal sounds. In fact we sometimes tune them out completely!

But we need to re-value the little sounds that they make, so that they understand their voice is important. If we don't notice these little sounds or respond right away, then their vocal attempts have nowhere to land. If we want to show them the power of their own voice, we can start right away by responding to these little sounds. It doesn't mean that we ignore the physical communication attempts, we just focus ourselves to notice the vocal sounds we are so used to screening out. One of the main things parents often notice when we look at videos together is exactly how much their child is trying to communicate with their voice, and how much they miss their attempts in real-time!

Now we know some of the basics, let's start with our first strategy.

3

Eye Level Positions

This is a vastly underestimated strategy and one that can have such a huge impact on children and bring out their best potential. This strategy done regularly offers your child the best chance at creating a connection which we know leads to more frequent communication.

So the very first thing we need to consider to set up communication for success is being opposite your child at eye level. Take a minute now to think about the positions you usually get into when playing, singing or reading with your child. I'm sure there are many times you are at eye level. But thinking now, do you think there are times when you are side by side when reading books or playing with toys? Or even behind them if the toys are stacked against the wall? If this is the case, can they see your face or your mouth? How easy do you think it would be for your child to tear themselves away from what they are doing to look towards you or include you in their play or interact with you?

There are a number of reasons why eye level positions are so important for speech and language:

1. It is easier for them to include you in their world. By just being in front of them at eye level, suddenly you are part of the game! There will be increased opportunities for them to interact or communicate with you.
2. They don't have to shift their attention away from what they are doing. We know that all children find this difficult - Think of calling their attention away from the TV or a device! So when we are opposite them at eye level, it is so much easier for them to notice us.
3. They get to see your face! They can notice what you are looking at, the shapes you make with your mouth and it is likely that your voice will reach them more clearly.
4. You get to see what they are looking at and interested in, moment by moment! If you're not able to see their face, you may miss some subtle clues about what they are thinking about. And this is important when we want to follow their interest and comment on what is fun for them.
5. The more opportunities you provide for communication, the more they get to *practice* and get better and better at communicating.

There is one caveat however: Some children do not like others in their personal space. So if this sounds like your child - perhaps they grumble, move away or turn their back on you - then you may need to place yourself a little further away at a distance that is comfortable for them. You will still be making a difference by being in front of them rather than at their side.

I do not advocate working on increasing eye contact, because for some children this can be physically uncomfortable. We do all the work, to get ourselves into the most favorable position to help them notice us and potentially want to engage with us. They don't need to make eye contact to feel connected to you, and you being present is enough for them to be aware and notice you.

Possible Positions

So what are the possible positions we should think to get ourselves into? You are likely using some of these positions already. But we don't often think of kneeling on the floor when a child is sitting on the couch, or lying on our elbows so that we can be a little lower than them when they are looking down at toys on the floor!

Let's look at some examples to help you think about positions you could get into when interacting with your child.

Consider eye level options when your child is on the sofa

When your child is sitting on the sofa, you can kneel down in front of the sofa where they sit. You will have a good chance of being at their eye level. Or you could both sit opposite each other on the couch as in the image on the right.

When reading a book with your child, you can hold it under your chin between you and your child. It means you'll be reading upside down, *but* your child can glance at you more easily to see your face and see the book at the same time. This means you are in the best position for them to learn from watching your face, while they enjoy the book. If your child doesn't enjoy books, that's fine. You will know what to do when they are ready.

Consider lying on your tummy, leaning on elbows, or having your child on your lap facing you

Lying on your elbows is a great way for you to get low down enough when your child is on the floor. Or they could straddle you or sit on your lap facing you when you sing songs and look at books together.

Ideas for eye level positions when out

When you are out and about, it is in some ways even more important to think about physically getting eye to eye, as you may be standing and much higher than your child's eye level. So lifting your child up, or getting on your knees will ensure that they will have the best chance to see your face when you are talking to them.

Eye level for fun games

Many children like games involving just people: like tickles, peekaboo or chasing. These naturally lend themselves to connection, because it is all about you and them and there is nothing else to capture their attention - *you* are the toy! Many children like cause-and-effect toys that need to be operated by someone else, like bubbles. These are ideal opportunities to get face to face on the floor so that you can be at eye level.

How to Arrange your Toy Furniture

The next thing you need to consider is what toy furniture you have, if any. Pull out children's tables or kitchen play sets away from the wall so that you can get behind them and be opposite your child, instead of side by side. You can see some examples below.

Consider options to get face to face with toy furniture or play equipment

Arranging Toys

You also need to consider the toys you have and how they are arranged. Often times we leave toys out and available for children to play with. This seems like a great idea! But too many toys can be distracting, and it's hard to physically move around with many obstructions on the floor. It can also be more difficult to get stuck in with one play activity: Sometimes children might flit from one thing to the next without really settling on anything specific.

You could consider taking some of the toys and putting them away. You can put toys on rotation so there are new toys to explore periodically. It is worth doing this as your child may not show interest in a particular toy now, but that can change! So putting toys on rotation gives you the chance to check in every few weeks and see if they have moved on and if they are ready for a previously ignored toy.

Too many toys out can also mean it will be harder for them to shift their attention to others and connect with others, especially if the toys are piled up in a corner of the room or against a wall. In this case they will be facing the wall as they play. So find ways to store toys in such a way that they can be brought out into the middle of the room. You may like to have a special play rug, which identifies a specific area for play. Then you can both sit on the rug with your child's chosen toys between you.

You could store toys in see-through boxes or containers, so that your child can decide what they want to play with each day. You may consider furniture with containers you can pull out when your child expresses an interest in playing with something. This creates lots of opportunities for you to talk about the toys and potentially make decisions together too!

Then tidy up time is a great daily routine when you can sing a 'clean up' song your child can enjoy and get involved with, if and when they are ready to.

4

Days 1 and 2: Eye Level Video Practice

This is your practice time, when you get to try out some of the things we have talked about! This is important because if you don't practice in a planned way, it is unlikely that you will use the strategy consistently and often enough for it to make a difference.

Do **_not_** continue until you have completed two days of practice. Follow these steps each in turn:

- First, spend some time preparing the room, including toys and toy furniture and equipment. Look at the area where your child usually plays. Do you need to put some toys on rotation? Are they against the wall and could you organize the toys differently based on some of the suggestions we discussed? Could you organise a play area where you can get opposite your child, perhaps on a cozy rug?

- Now that you have set up your room for success, grab your phone. Have someone to video you, or set it up somewhere where it will capture both you and your child in the frame. Spend 2-3 minutes interacting with your child. You'll be focusing on getting into the eye level positions we have talked about. Refresh your memory by looking at the pictures. And write down some of the positions you plan to get into, knowing where your child likes to be.

- After the 3 minutes of interaction are up, review your recorded video and note what happened. Did getting at eye level have any effect on your child? Did you get to follow them around the room? Did you notice more engagement in any way? Were there other changes you noticed? Was your child uncomfortable and did you have to move a little further away?

- Don't move on until you have completed the two days practice: Repeat this exercise at least 2 to 3 times today and tomorrow: a total of 4-6 times over the two days. This will help you get into the mindset of eye level positions and help you to think of using the positions in your everyday interactions with your child.

The next strategy we will look at will help you slow down so you can get an idea of what possible new fun things you could talk about.

5

Pausing

Pausing is something that we often don't do enough of. We feel so under pressure to 'teach' our children, and we feel that any silence is a missed opportunity to teach something new! But the reality is that your child needs silence just as much as hearing language.

Again, there are so many reasons why pausing is so important:

We usually lead interactions and try to 'teach' something new, but the problem with this is that we can't 'teach' language in the same way as teaching how to brush one's teeth, or wash our hands. Communication is best addressed within natural fun activities that children really enjoy. And *we* don't determine what is fun for them - *they* do!

When we lead, we are missing an opportunity for a child to lead and show us what they are thinking of, and what they find fun, moment by moment. Their attention can flit from what we assume they are focused on to literally anything, and we need to be ready so that we can comment on whatever new momentary thing has captured their attention!

When we pause, we are giving ourselves the gift of time to watch and figure out what it is that they are interested in or experiencing.

When children take the initiative or find something fun and then if we join in, they learn quicker and it sticks better: They are picking their own fun things to do, and often, learning happens when engaging in 'unconventional' or unexpected play.

Conversely, it is more difficult for them to learn when we bring our agenda to the table. They are usually less invested in it than we are! When we lead, we may happen to land on the thing they like by chance! But we are also missing opportunities to find new leads and new things they might like - that *they* choose. They can usually tell when we are trying to 'teach' them something too!

We usually say too much, with too many questions and too many comments back to back. The impact of our constant chatter is that a child probably won't have enough time to process each comment we say. They may even hear our chat as a 'mush of noise'. They may screen out our voices, or our constant chatter may even annoy them! Some children go into a 'doesn't apply to me' mode when we narrate. When this happens we lose the to-and-fro nature of communication.

On the other hand, if you are naturally a quiet person, you may need to become aware of whether you need to say more! You'll have an idea about how to keep a nice flow going in our next video practice section.

Here are some practical tips to get you into the mindset of pausing:

Sit quietly now and count slowly to 30 in your mind. This is how long you need to wait when you sit down with your child. It may feel like a long time - and that's the point! We need to stop leading and leave enough space for *them* to start doing something, instead of us coming in and trying to find something for them to do or something to teach them! When they start doing something, you can be sure it is going to be something fun for them, because they have chosen it. This is where the learning can start.

Write 'Pause' on several stickies and put them on the wall wherever you usually interact with your child. This will help you to remember to hold back and pause more often.

6

Days 3 and 4: Pausing Video Practice

- Get ready and set your phone to video you interacting with your child. ***Don't move on*** until you have completed two days of practice: You will practice this exercise and video yourself at least 2- 3 times today and tomorrow, making a total of 4-6 times over the two days. Set up your phone to capture both of you in the frame and record yourself and your child for 2-3 minutes. When you go to your child, sit quietly with them for 30 seconds. Do not be tempted to say anything! This is the time for your child to feel relaxed with no pressure to do or say anything, and for you to simply be present.

- After the 30 seconds are up and you know what your child is interested in, you can comment once excitedly on what it is that is happening. After your one comment, pause again for 15 seconds. Do not be tempted to say another comment until you have counted to 15! As you pause, watch your child for any signals they send you so you can smile and nod. React physically by getting the things they want, or to other requests they may have. Don't worry too much about what to say yet. We'll focus on that in our final strategy.

- Replay your video after the 3 minutes recording are up and watch yourself and your child carefully.

- Was your waiting at the start as long as you imagined it was? Or did you only wait a few seconds before launching in with a comment? Did you accidentally lead the activity? Did your child have the space to initiate something they wanted to do?

- What did you notice about what your child was interested in? Did it vary moment by moment? Did you spot any attention grabbers you could say something about?

- Did they interact differently with you than usual? In what way? Did they initiate interaction with you?

Take your reflections as clues for what helps your child to communicate more with you. My experience is that most parents find their child usually interacts with them more when they stay more quiet and present, when they join in with fun activities

DAYS 3 AND 4: PAUSING VIDEO PRACTICE

determined by their child moment by moment, and when they keep pausing after each comment.

If you have completed your two days practice and you're ready to move on, let's talk about what to say in more detail in the next chapter.

If you are finding this book useful, you can help other parents find it by leaving a review here:https://www.amazon.com/review/create-review/?ie=UTF8&channel=glance-detail&asin=B0CNTYTD51

Leave a Review!

7

Modeling Without Expectation

'*Modeling without expectation*' means that you comment about what your child is thinking or interested in, without any expectation for them to do or say anything back.

Now you might ask: 'So how are they going to learn to communicate better then?'. The reality is that children need to hear words in natural comments over and over, many, many times before they can understand what they mean.

Once they understand what the words mean, then your child may be in a position to start attempting to say them, when they are ready. We cannot force this step, this is a process your child is completely in charge of.

So our role is to model the language in context and say what they might want to say, what they are thinking of - for them - so that they can learn the meaning of the words and phrases. You have already worked hard to follow your child in whatever activity they find fun, even if this was unconventional play. You were looking for opportunities to connect over whatever caught their interest, so that you could comment on that. Then you kept practicing pausing after each comment so they could process what you said. Let's talk in more detail now about what we mean by 'comments'.

As parents, we are primed to 'teach'. We want to expose our children to new fun experiences so that they will learn from them. But as a side effect of our 'teacher' role, we also tend to ask a lot of questions: ...

- *'What's this?'*
- *'Who's that?'*
- *'Where does this go?'*

The problem with asking lots of questions is that they feel a bit like a test to see what they know... By asking questions, we set up communication as something that is hard. We know what this feels like because we felt a bit like this when we had to take tests in school or college... We really don't like them! It is likely your child will eventually have a similar experience and likely won't really enjoy all the questions you ask them.

For children who are not yet talking, or only have a few words, they may not yet understand question words, so our questions have nowhere to land: they won't be answered, so why ask them?

We know that children learn best when they are having fun, so what can we do instead of asking testy questions that may not get answered?

We can comment. This means using statements. We can use comments or statements to talk about what is happening, how we feel, or about something we find intriguing or interesting!

What types of questions should we avoid?

'Wh' Questions

It is easy to tell that 'Wh' words are questions, like 'Who', 'What', 'Where' and 'Why'. We also include 'How' in this category of questions:

- 'Who's turn is it?'
- 'What's that funny noise?'
- 'Where will we put the dinosaur?'
- 'Why is he sad?'
- 'How did he make it?'

It could be that your child is already indicating an answer by pointing or saying something - which is great! But if your focus is mostly on questions, then you are missing opportunities for your child to hear and learn language they could say when they are ready. You're also missing opportunities for your child to pair what they hear with what they see or what they are experiencing in that moment. More missed opportunities include those where your child to initiate spontaneously, instead of responding to prompted questions.

Yes/No Questions

Another flag is if you notice that you start with 'Do' or 'Is' or 'Are', because this means you are asking a Yes/No question!

- 'Do you want it?'
- 'Is it red?'
- 'Are you hungry?'

Yes/No questions are not bad in themselves, but the only answer your child can give is either 'yes' or 'no', so they tend to be conversation stoppers. When we say a comment instead, it leaves the possibilities open to say anything at all!

Tag Questions

Other questions are called 'tag' questions. These are the ones that we add onto comments:

- 'It's red, *isn't it?*'
- 'I'm eating the biggest piece, *aren't I?*'
- 'You like that one, *don't you?*'

One problem with Tag questions is how they take away from comments by turning them into Yes/No questions, and as we just mentioned, Yes/No Questions tend to be conversation stoppers.

The other problem about Tag questions relates to how children process language: the final word or words you say are the ones that your child is most likely to hear most clearly and therefore process most easily. So when you say a comment with a tag question, your comment is lost and your child is more likely to process the last thing they year - the tag question! From our examples, here is what your child will be most likely to focus on and process:

- *'Isn't it?'*
- *'Aren't I?'*
- *'Don't you?'*

So this is wasted real estate! We want to use that last word position for meaningful and relevant words that your child can process and learn.

Comments

So what kind of comments are we talking about? The type of comments we model depends on:

- What they are interested in - we must comment on what they are experiencing in that very moment. What is it that they are seeing, feeling, or thinking in that moment? Then pause.... This is so that they can link the words you have just said with their own sensory experience or thoughts. Over time they will learn what your words mean, because you are offering them at the right moment with lots of time to listen and process.

- Your child's communication stage will have a bearing on the way you phrase your comments. A child who is not yet talking needs a combination of sound effects ('Boo!' 'Vroom vroom!') single words and short phrases. Whereas a child who is already saying lots of single words and some phrases will need to hear more phrases.

- A general guideline for the length of comments for most children is: *2-4 syllables*. This is short enough to be processed and long enough to give them some grammar to hear for when they are ready.

- If your child is a non-speaker, or if they frequently repeat what others say, then it is helpful to 'be their voice' and offer comments that are from their point of view, using *'I'* or *'Me'* as if you were them. *'I'm so hungry!' 'Help me, Mommy!'*

Tips For Commenting

Good starter words to ensure you are using a comment (rather than a question) are:

- 'Let's': *Let's go to the park! Let's get a snack! Let's go out! Let's play!*
- 'We': *We did it! We're gonna make it! We can play now!*
- 'That': *That's so cool! That's a big one!*
- 'It's / This': *It's / This is so much fun! It's / This is a train!*
- 'There('s)': *There's Daddy! There are two ducks!*

This is not an exhaustive list so feel free to add your own starter words once they are not 'Wh' questions or 'Yes/No' questions!'

You can also consider using *Commands*:

- 'Put it in!'
- 'Take it out!'
- 'Tidy up!'

Do not ask your child to 'Tell me about…' or 'Say ——-!'. Asking a child to say something places demands on them, even if they are well able to say it. It gives them the sense that communication is hard and there is a 'right' answer. It also does not reflect natural conversation and will likely take away from all the work you are doing to build communication trust with your child.

There are simple ways to help build your child's trust in you as a communication partner and to help them feel like communication is easy, so that they will want to do lots more of it. We'll cover this in the next section.

Listen Acknowledge Model and Show/Give

Finally, let's talk about how to keep the conversation going so that you develop a nice flow or rhythm to your interactions back and forth. This strategy also helps to build communication trust, all while making your child feel like communication is effortless.

We have already talked about following your child to wherever the fun takes them, then commenting and pausing. But what happens if your child tries to communicate something to you?

We take a simple 'Listen Acknowledge, Model and Show/Give' approach.

Because you have been pausing and watching your child more, you may notice your child making efforts to communicate with you. This may be physically, by moving their body, changing their facial expression, and going near what they want. Or it could be by making vocal sounds, or it could be by pushing your hand, bringing things to you, moving you in some way. It could involve looking at you expectantly or pointing to something. Or it could involve words.

All of these ways are valid ways to communicate. So when you are watching and listening, acknowledge what they have communicated in any way on their first attempt. '

'Okay! Wow! Yes! Uh huh!' and nodding your head are all really nice ways to acknowledge your child's message.

MODELING WITHOUT EXPECTATION

Sometimes you may not know what they want to tell you. In this case the best thing to do is often to nod appreciatively, smile and give a non-committal comment or 'banter' like *'Wow! Really? I didn't know that!'.* You can also try repeating what you heard them say, back to them in a fun way.

If your child is insistent on communicating something specific and you don't understand and you have tried encouraging them to show you or tell another way, then you have to acknowledge the misunderstanding. You can say *'I'm sorry, I don't know!'.* They may still get upset, but at least they will know you are trying your best to understand, and you'll have acknowledged their attempt.

If you do notice something in their voice, or actions that are communicating something that you can interpret, then now is the time to acknowledge their message and model something that relates to their message! Add a facial expression, hand gesture or body language. Here are some examples:

'Yes, you're right!.... It is fun!' (add a body gesture for 'this' like putting your arms out with your palms up)
   'Wow! You made a huge tower!' (add an action for 'huge')
   'Hungry?.... Okay, let's get a snack!' (put out your hand as an invitation to go)
   'Yes! I see it!.... There's that bird again!' (point to the bird)
   'Uh huh!.... That's so yummy!' (rub your tummy)
   'Sure!.... We can do that!' (nod and a thumbs up)
   'I need help!.... Help me, Daddy!' (use your facial expression and hands out to show a natural gesture for *'help'*)

When you use these conversational comments and natural gestures, your child is learning so much about the meaning of what you say in context, the emotional intonation or melody of your voice, and linking your words to the meaning - because you're talking about what they are thinking and feeling! You're also giving some nonverbal clues to help them understand your words when you use your face, hands and body.

This strategy works especially well if your child says one word that you understand, and you want to respond with something relevant. Use the 2-4 syllable guide to help you. It's not a drama if you use 5 or more syllables, but 7 or 8 could be a little too long for them to process.

Your child may not use words yet, or they may not be combining many words yet, but you are laying the foundations for them to learn the vocabulary and information they need to understand how conversations go back and forth. Your comments will relate to what's happening right now, without feeling 'testy' and without narrating in the background. You'll be relevant and meaningful! Your comments will intrigue and interest your child because you'll be picking up on their favorite things! They may switch off if you try to narrate or teach them about the 'green car, 'blue car, or 'red car'. But their ears might perk up a lot more and they might connect with you when you notice them playing with a wheel and you add the words 'round and round and round' in an excited tone. Your pauses will give them the time they need to process what you have said. The learning may not be immediately obvious, and that's okay!

You help them understand their world and their thoughts when you show them what you are both talking about. If they have asked for something and you can give it, then you are giving it to show that you have understood. These are powerful ways for your child to feel heard and valued.

By using comments, you are also showing them that communication is more than just asking for our immediate needs: it is also about sharing information with each other. When we model a range of relevant comments, commands (and questions when they are ready), we are setting them up for successful communication later. They get to hear how one comment leads to another related comment. And this reflects what conversation back and forth is all about.

8

Days 5 and 6: Modeling Without Expectation Video Practice

- Get ready to video yourself for 2-3 minutes again! You will try this exercise at least 2-3 times today and tomorrow, for a total of 4-6 times over the two days. This time you are going to practice identifying what your child is interested in moment by moment. Their state of being, and what they might be interested in. Then check the starter word list and think of what you could say in a natural way that fits the situation - their thoughts, feelings, their actions, what happens that is interesting or intriguing for them! Add a gesture where possible. If they have requested something, give it to them. Stay quiet for at least 10-15 seconds, until you find something interesting to comment on. Avoid saying comments back to back.

- Remember to video yourself playing together, face to face, watching your child, following what your child wants to do and what they

DAYS 5 AND 6: MODELING WITHOUT EXPECTATION VIDEO PRACTICE

find fun - this could be tickles, peekaboo, chase, book, toy play, swings, slides, sensory fun. But could equally be the sound of the cars going by, the feeling of the wind on their face, the warmth of the sun, the texture of the leaves on the ground.

- After the recording part is over, watch your video back carefully. Did you wait long enough or did you start to take over the conversation? Did you manage to follow your child's fun or did you start to introduce or teach your own ideas again? Did you comment on an intriguing part of the activity your child chose? Or did you comment on their state of being (emotions / hunger / thirst etc..) Or did you comment on what your child might be thinking? What impact did this have on the interaction? Did you feel more connected? Did your child notice you more? Did they initiate interaction or communication with you more? What are your takeaways from this exercise? What do you want to practice more of? What are you doing well?

We have now covered all three of the easy strategies to make a difference to your child's interaction, communication or language skills, depending on their communication level. Well done for getting this far! I'm sure you are seeing some changes already within yourself, now that you are becoming your child's ideal communication partner! Sometimes it may seem like there is nothing happening, but don't lose courage, you are doing the right things to help your child progress. You may not be seeing it manifest outwardly yet, but your child is learning all sorts of things on the inside that you can't see yet!

When you have completed your two days practice and reflection tasks, we will focus on bringing everything you have learned together, on what will be the final day of our 7 day practice!

9

Day 7: Pulling It All Together

Congratulations on making it to day 7! This is where you get to practice all your strategies at the one time. This can be tricky as there is a lot to think about! You have come a long way in a short space of time, and if you have done the practice every day so far, then this should be relatively easy for you.

If you didn't get to do the practice alongside each day, go back and practice each day's exercises separately. My experience is that it is not realistic to practice everything together from the get-go. Splitting up each strategy and practicing them independently works much better and gives you the confidence to keep going.

When parents try to practice everything all at the one time, it can become overwhelming and they can quickly become discouraged. So make sure to only try this exercise once you have completed all the previous exercises.

You will record yourself again and this time focus on practicing all these strategies:

1. Eye Level Position
2. Pausing
3. Modeling without Expectation
4. Listen Acknowledge Model and Show/Give

Start by sitting quietly with your child. Wait at least 30 seconds and say nothing. Just watch your child. If your child communicates something during those 30 seconds, you can **Listen and Acknowledge** by smiling and nodding. Don't comment yet. Just let the events unfold and see where your child brings you in terms of fun!

Once you have noticed what your child is interested in or intrigued by (which remember may not be what we think of as a 'conventional' activity), check the starter word list and make *ONE* **Comment** that best fits the situation (with a gesture) then pause for at least 15 seconds to see what happens next.

If your child communicates something, Listen to what they say or do, then Acknowledge by smiling/nodding or using an expression appropriate to the situation. Then check your word starter list and make a **Comment** that links with what they are thinking or feeling - ***not*** with what ***you*** are thinking! Let's recap some examples:

- 'That feels spiky!'
- 'I'm so hungry!'
- 'This is red!'
- 'I like that one!'
- 'Let's play!'
- 'That's funny!'

DAY 7: PULLING IT ALL TOGETHER

Keep repeating this process - watching for intriguing things or for your child's communication attempts then *Listen Acknowledge, Model and Show/Give.*

That's it! It sounds simple and you may think that you've been doing this all along, but when you focus on doing these strategies in such a planned way, you become totally present. You are listening, really paying attention, tuning into your child in a way that you can only do when you are truly focused on them and not focusing on teaching anything specific anymore.

When you tune into them and comment and pause in the way we have learned in this book, you are working on so much more than communication: You are building communication trust with your child, you are validating them and helping them realize the importance of their voice. They are learning about their own importance and self-agency in the world - the ability to express their wants, likes and dislikes. This has a huge impact on how they view themselves, their identity and their thinking skills in the long run.

10

Conclusion

You made it! You have spent a full 7 days working on your relationship with your child, and on building healthy communication habits. You are now a supportive communication partner for your child. The interactions you have with them are relevant, at the right communication level for them, without placing undue demands on them, and you are setting up each interaction for communication success. You're accepting their first communication attempt and you're commenting less but with more meaning to your child, so that they will learn little things each time you interact and communicate with them.

To maintain your new skills into the future, keep recording yourself for 2-3 minutes a day, or every other day, for the next 4 weeks. Watch your recordings back right away, and follow the Day 7 prompt questions and reflect on what you could have done differently. This will help you transfer what you have learned into long term habits and establish a new communication style that you will naturally and effortlessly use in every interactions you have with your child.

CONCLUSION

Don't forget to sign up for your free **tip sheet** below, to get information on how to sign up for a **free 15 minute call** with Carolyn to see if a **coaching consultation** on these and other strategies would be of benefit to you and your child.

Sign Up for the Free Tip Sheet Here!

If you are finding this book useful, you can help other parents find it by leaving a review here:https://www.amazon.com/review/create-review/?ie=UTF8&channel=glance-detail&asin=B0CNTYTD51

Leave a Review!

11

References

Blanc, M. (2012). "*Natural Language Acquisition: The Journey from Echolalia to Self-Generated Language.*" Communication Development Center.

Finestack, L.H. and Fey, M.E. (2013). '*Evidence-Based Language Intervention Approaches for Young Talkers*'. In Rescorla, L.A. and Dale, P.S. (eds.). *(2013). Late Talkers: Language Development, Interventions, and Outcomes.* Paul H Brookes Publishing Co., Baltimore, MD.

Law J, Charlton J, Dockrell J, Gascoigne M, McKean C, Theakston A. (2017). '*Early Language Development: Needs, provision and intervention for pre-school children from socio-economically disadvantaged backgrounds. London Education Endowment Foundation*'. Public Health England.

Law. J. et al. (2020). '*Best Start in Speech, Language and Communication: Supporting Evidence*', PHE publications PHE gateway number: GW-1162. Taken from: https://assets.publishing.service.gov.uk/media/5f9be9c4 8fa8f57f3b4cb075/BSSLC_Supporting-evidence.pdf

REFERENCES

Ní Choisdealbha A., Attaheri A., Rocha S., Mead N., Olawole Scott H., Brusini P., Gibbon S., Boutris P., Grey C., Hines D., Williams I., Flanagan S. A., Goswami U., (2023) *'Neural Phase Angle From Two Months When Tracking Speech And Non-Speech Rhythm Linked To Language Performance From 12 To 24 Months'*. Volume 243, August 2023: Brain and Language.

Webb, C. J. (2023). *'A Parent's Guide To Early Communication; Jump-Start Your Child's Interaction and Language Skills Towards First Words and Phrases; 7 Powerful Strategies With Transformative Video Exercises',* DIY Speech Therapy Publications.

Useful Websites for Additional Information:

www.diyspeechtherapy.com

www.meaningfulspeech.com

https://communicationdevelopmentcenter.com

SLT Top Tips for supporting Early Communication development

www.ingramcontent.com/pod-product-compliance
Lightning Source LLC
Chambersburg PA
CBHW071039080526
44587CB00015B/2691